Make it in a Jar

CUPCAKES, PIES, COOKIES & MORE
MADE IN A JAR

Contents

Introduction   4

Bake in a jar   10

Make in a jar   34

Take in a jar   56

Index   78

Introduction

When you hear the terms 'preserving jars' and 'mason jars,' you may picture your grandmother in a flowery pinny bottling jams and marmalades. Generations of thrifty housewives, resourceful cooks and green-fingered gardeners have used these tempered glass beauties to put up the season's bounty to last through cold winters. But there's a trend afoot that has elevated these timeless vessels to do-it-all status and they have become *de rigueur* in the modern kitchen. Simply put, preserving jars are as retro-chic as they are undeniably practical.

They are attractive, come in a multitude of shapes and sizes, and can go from the larder to the oven to the freezer to the fridge and back again. Use them as serving dishes and containers for lunchbox salads, cooking vessels for cakes, pies, even pizza, or as gift wrapping for cookie and soup mixes. Bake mini cakes in small jars, tuck them in the freezer, and you'll always have a fancy dessert at the ready for unexpected guests. A jar of brownie or hot chocolate mix is the perfect gift for a surprise Christmas guest. And batches of ready-to-make pancake mixture or ready-to-bake pasta with rich, creamy cheese sauce will make welcome gifts for you and your family on busy days when you don't have a lot of time to cook a meal.

In short, what can't you do with a mason jar?

SELECTING JARS

If you plan to use the jars for long-term storage or for cooking, be sure to buy authentic preserving or mason jars, which are made of tempered, heat-resistant glass and come with lids that are equipped with channels coated with a sealing compound.

Some preserving-jar lids are in two pieces – a flat lid with a sealing rim and a metal band to hold it in place – while others are one-piece lids that screw right onto the jar in one go.

Since we're not concerned here with preserving food in the long term, any type of preserving jars and lids will work very well for our purposes.

For simplicity's sake, the recipes in this book use two sizes/shapes of jars: 225-ml/8-fl oz wide-mouthed jars and 475-ml/16-fl oz wide-mouthed jars. Buy a dozen of each of these sizes and you'll be prepared to make any of the recipes in this book.

We chose the wide-mouthed jars, which have straight sides instead of 'shoulders', both because they are the most practical for use as serving vessels and because they are safe to use in the freezer (this is because liquid expands in all directions when it freezes, so even though there may be headspace above the shoulder of a normal-mouthed jar, the expansion of the liquid upon freezing could still break the jar).

Many of the recipes, however, will work equally well in normal-mouthed jars of the same size as long as you're not planning to freeze them. If you already have a store of preserving jars you'd like to put to use, by all means go ahead and use them.

The most important thing is that the jars you choose are in good shape, free from chips or cracks.

HOW TO USE CANNING JARS

Canning jars can be used in myriad different ways. In the first section of this book, we focus on dishes that are cooked and served right in the jars, from pizza to tarts and pies to cakes. These recipes make good use of the jars' heat-resistant qualities and also take advantage of their usefulness in creating pre-portioned individual servings perfect for entertaining, and packing for a picnic or other on-the-go meals.

In the second section, we offer dishes that use the jars as serving vessels, showing off the beautiful layering of colours and textures in dishes – Red Velvet Cupcakes layered with fluffy buttercream, Orange Panna Cotta with blackberry compote, Quinoa Salad with strawberries, almonds, green onions and mint. Again, these dishes are ideal for entertaining, packing to eat on the go, or for giving.

In the third and final section, we use the jars as gift wrapping for festive foods made specifically for giving, from Red Lentil Soup Mix to Blueberry Pancake Mix and ready-to-bake cookie dough.

Each of these applications takes advantage of the jars' see-through nature to show off interesting colours and textures in the food, as well as their unique ability to be used in the hot oven, chilled, frozen and even used for serving and transporting foods.

TIPS FOR SUCCESS

Preserving jars are surprisingly versatile, but they function a bit differently from the usual cooking, serving and storage vessels. The recipes in this book have all been developed specifically for cooking, serving or storing in preserving jars, but if you are adapting a standard recipe to these applications, a bit of trial and error is unavoidable. Remember that things will cook at different rates in the jars than in your usual cooking vessels, and you may need to practise your layering technique a little to get just the visual impact you're hoping for.

To clean the jars, simply wash them by hand with washing-up liquid in hot water, or put them in the dishwasher. If using the jars for long-term storage, it's a good idea to sterilize them as well by submerging them in boiling water for 10–15 minutes before filling them.

When choosing recipes to make or serve in jars, think visually. Look for dishes that include a variety of colours and textures that can be layered in creative ways. Brightly coloured fruits and vegetables and earthy nuts and seeds are all wonderful for creating stunning dishes.

When freezing food in jars, be sure to use the straight-sided, wide-mouthed jars and leave about 1 cm/½ inch of headroom at the top to allow for the expansion that takes place when liquid freezes. If you use normal-mouthed jars (with shoulders), you should fill them only about two-thirds full to avoid potential breakage.

Ready-to-bake cookie dough freezes quite well and the cookies can be removed from the jar and put straight into a preheated oven for baking. Thaw other frozen foods by placing them either in the refrigerator overnight or on a work surface for several hours. Cakes freeze quite well, but they should be frozen before icing and iced after they have thawed.

In today's kitchen, preserving jars function as far more than just utilitarian vessels for long-term storage and preservation of fruits and vegetables. They offer a whimsical way to cook, serve and make gifts of food that will delight your family and friends. Have fun with the process and be creative with the visual opportunities the jars afford. Even your grandmother would be tickled pink to see the imaginative uses to which her boring old preserving jars are put these days.

BAKE

Bake

Preserving jars are ideal vessels for baking individual, single servings. Because they are made of heat-resistant tempered glass, the jars won't shatter in the oven and, in fact, baking in them is similar to baking in ceramic ramekins. And, as with ramekins, you save time on the washing-up by serving in the same vessel you've cooked in. Even better, with preserving jars you can pop a lid on the food and take it along for a picnic in the park or store it to use another day.

Perhaps best of all, preserving jars really show off all the colours and textures of layered food, as in the rainbow cakes that have been all the rage in the blogosphere (and, of course, we've got a version here, too). But it's not just desserts that can be baked in jars. Try baked pasta dishes like Macaroni Cheese, savoury tarts like our Asparagus Tart or, believe it or not, even pizza!

Many of these recipes can be stored in the refrigerator or freezer either before or after cooking. Some foods, such as our Berry Cobbler or Macaroni Cheese, are best frozen prior to cooking and then popped, still frozen, directly into a hot oven, while others, like cakes, are best stored after baking, but before icing. Thaw cakes for a few hours on a work surface and ice just before serving. For your convenience, each recipe includes instructions for storing and thawing or reheating in the 'Cook's Tips' section.

Cooking in jars isn't complicated, but it is a bit different from cooking in the usual metal baking tins. Smaller portions will cook more quickly than larger portions. On the other hand, cooking in glass can take slightly longer than cooking in metal. Trial and error is par for the course when you are adapting a regular recipe to be cooked in jars. Of course, the recipes here have all been developed for and tested in jars, but you might want to plan for a test run if you are cooking a standard recipe in jars for the first time.

Rainbow Cakes

Preserving jars are perfect for showing off the pretty rainbow layers of these cute little cakes. A sweet cloud of frosting and colourful hundreds and thousands are just the right finishing touch.

MAKES: 6 small jars

PREP TIME 45 minutes
COOK TIME 24 minutes

INGREDIENTS:

non-stick baking spray, for greasing

200 g/7 oz plain flour

1½ tsp baking powder

¼ tsp salt

115 g/4 oz unsalted butter, at room temperature

200 g/7 oz caster sugar

2 tsp vanilla extract

4 large egg whites

125 ml/4 fl oz milk

red, yellow, green and blue gel food colouring

multi-coloured hundreds and thousands, to decorate

Frosting

3 egg whites

175 g/6 oz sugar

225 g/8 oz unsalted butter, at room temperature

1 tbsp vanilla extract

1. Preheat the oven to 180°C/350°F/Gas Mark 4. Spray the insides of six 225-ml/8-fl oz wide-mouthed preserving jars with baking spray and place the jars on a Swiss roll tin.

2. To make the cakes, put the flour, baking powder and salt into a medium-sized bowl and mix to combine.

3. Put the butter and sugar into a large bowl and beat with an electric mixer set on high speed until pale and fluffy. Add the vanilla extract, then add the egg whites, one at a time, beating after each addition until incorporated. Scrape down the side of the bowl, add half the flour mixture and beat on medium speed until incorporated. Scrape down the side of the bowl, add the milk and beat until incorporated. Scrape down the side of the bowl, add the remaining flour mixture and beat until just incorporated.

4. Divide the batter between six small bowls. Colour one bowl of batter red, using 8–10 drops of red food colouring. Colour one bowl orange with 8 drops of yellow food colouring and 4 drops of red. Colour one bowl yellow with 8 drops of yellow food colouring. Colour one bowl green with 8 drops of green food colouring. Colour one bowl blue with 8 drops of blue food colouring. Colour one bowl purple with 8 drops of red food colouring and 4 drops of blue.

5. Spoon the batter into the prepared jars, one colour at a time, starting with purple. Drop a tablespoonful into each jar and smooth it out with the back of the spoon so that it covers the entire base of the jar. Divide all the purple batter between the jars before moving on to the next colour. Repeat with the blue, green, yellow, orange and red batters, in that order with the remaining bowls of batter. Bake in the preheated oven for 22–24 minutes, until a cocktail stick inserted into the centre of a cake comes out clean. Remove from the oven and leave to cool.

6. Meanwhile, to make the frosting, heat some water in the base of a double boiler until just simmering. Put the egg whites and sugar into the top of the double boiler and mix to combine. Set over the simmering water (the pan should be touching the water) and whisk constantly for about 5 minutes, until the sugar is completely dissolved (carefully dip in a

To store the cakes, follow the recipe until the cooked cakes have cooled to room temperature. Do not prepare the frosting. Seal the jars with their lids and store the cakes in the refrigerator for up to 5 days or in the freezer for up to 3 months. To serve, bring the cakes to room temperature, prepare the frosting as directed, and frost the cakes just before serving.

thumb and finger and rub together; if there are no grains left, the sugar is fully dissolved) and the mixture is warm. Remove from the heat and, using an electric mixer fitted with a whisk attachment, beat the mixture on high speed for about 5 minutes, until it holds stiff, glossy peaks. Add the butter, 1–2 tablespoons at a time, and beat until the mixture holds stiff peaks. Add the vanilla extract and beat until just combined. Spoon the frosting into a piping bag fitted with your favourite tip.

7. When the cakes are completely cool, pipe the frosting onto them (if the cake has risen over the tops of the jars, remove some of it before topping with frosting). Sprinkle over the hundreds and thousands and serve the cakes at room temperature.

★ Cook's Tips ★

The uncooked cake batter can be kept in the refrigerator for 2-3 days or in the freezer for up to 1 month. When you have put the batter into the jars seal them tightly with their lids and place in the refrigerator or freezer. When ready to bake, remove the lids and proceed with the recipe. If frozen, add 10-15 minutes to the cooking time.

These tart yet sweet cakes are perfectly delightful on their own, but feel free to add a dollop of lightly sweetened whipped cream if you're feeling indulgent.

Lemon Drizzle

MAKES: 6 small jars

 PREP TIME 15 minutes
COOK TIME 30 minutes

INGREDIENTS:

200 g/7 oz plain flour

1½ tsp baking powder

¼ tsp salt

170 g/5¾ oz unsalted butter, at room temperature, plus extra for greasing

200 g/7 oz caster sugar

2 large eggs

finely grated zest and juice of 1 lemon

sweetened whipped cream, to serve (optional)

Glaze
50 g/1¾ oz sugar

juice of 1 lemon

1. Preheat the oven to 180°C/350°F/Gas Mark 4. Grease six 225-ml/8-fl oz wide-mouthed preserving jars and place them on a Swiss roll tin.

2. Put the flour, baking powder and salt into a medium-sized bowl and mix to combine.

3. Put the butter and sugar into a large bowl and beat with an electric mixer until pale and fluffy. Add the eggs, one at a time, beating after each addition until incorporated. Scrape down the side of the bowl, add the lemon zest and half the flour mixture and beat until well combined. Add the lemon juice and beat until incorporated. Scrape down the side of the bowl, add the remaining flour mixture and mix until just incorporated.

4. Divide the batter between the prepared jars and bake in the preheated oven for about 30 minutes, until a cocktail stick inserted in the centre comes out clean.

5. Remove from the oven and immediately poke several holes into each cake using a skewer or similar implement. To make the glaze, sprinkle 1 teaspoon of the sugar over the top of each cake. Add the lemon juice to the remaining sugar and stir until well combined. Spoon the mixture over the tops of the cakes. Serve warm or at room temperature, with whipped cream, if using.

2.

4.

5.

S'mores Cakes

Preserving jars are a much tidier and more convenient, but equally fun, way to serve this classic campfire treat.

MAKES: 8 small jars

 PREP TIME 30 minutes
COOK TIME 47 minutes

INGREDIENTS:

Base
115 g/4 oz digestive biscuits, broken into pieces

75 g/2¾ oz sugar

115 g/4 oz unsalted butter, melted, plus extra for greasing

Cakes
125 g/4½ oz plain flour

60 g/2¼ oz cocoa powder

1½ tsp baking powder

¼ tsp salt

115 g/4 oz unsalted butter, at room temperature

200 g/7 oz caster sugar

2 tsp vanilla extract

2 large eggs

125 ml/4 fl oz double cream

40 g/1½ oz mini plain chocolate chips or chopped plain chocolate

32 large marshmallows

1. Preheat the oven to 180°C/350°F/Gas Mark 4. Grease eight 225-ml/8-fl oz wide-mouthed preserving jars and place them on a Swiss roll tin.

2. To make the base, pulse the biscuits in a food processor until they are reduced to coarse crumbs. Add the sugar and butter and pulse until just combined.

3. Spoon about 2 tablespoons of the mixture into each of the prepared jars, using your thumb to flatten it into the base and up the sides. Bake in the preheated oven for about 12 minutes, until puffed and beginning to turn golden brown.

4. To make the cakes, put the flour, cocoa powder, baking powder and salt into a medium-sized bowl.

5. Put the butter and sugar into a large bowl and cream together with an electric mixer. Add the vanilla extract, then add the eggs, one at a time, beating after each addition until incorporated. Add half the flour mixture and beat until incorporated. Add the cream and beat until incorporated. Add the remaining flour mixture and beat until incorporated. Stir in the chocolate chips.

6. Scoop the batter into the prepared jars and bake in the preheated oven for about 30 minutes, until a cocktail stick inserted into the centre of a cake comes out almost clean.

7. Increase the oven temperature to 240°C/475°F/Gas Mark 9 and press 4 marshmallows into the top of each jar. Return the cakes to the oven and bake for a further 5–7 minutes, until the marshmallows are soft and lightly browned. Remove from the oven and leave to cool for a few minutes before serving. Serve warm.

3.

6.

7.

★ Cook's Tips ★

To store the cakes, follow the recipe up to step 6 then let the cakes cool to room temperature. Seal the jars with their lids and store the cakes in the refrigerator for up to 5 days or in the freezer for up to 3 months. To serve, preheat the oven to 240°C/475°F/Gas Mark 9, bring the cakes to room temperature, top with the marshmallows and heat as directed until the marshmallows are golden.

★ Cook's Tips ★

Assemble the pies and freeze in the lidded jars for up to 3 months.
To serve, remove the lids and place the pies on a Swiss roll tin in
a cold oven and heat the oven to 220°C/425°F/Gas Mark 7. Bake
for 20 minutes, then reduce the temperature to 190°C/375°F/Gas
Mark 5 and bake for 35–40 minutes, until cooked through. Let cool.

It's hard to believe that so few ingredients can make a dessert so delicious, delightful and portable.

Apple Pies

MAKES: 6 small jars

PREP TIME 15 minutes
COOK TIME 45–50 minutes

INGREDIENTS:

400 g/14 oz ready-made shortcrust pastry

375 g/13 oz peeled and cored Bramley apples, diced

1 tbsp lemon juice

65 g/2¾ oz granulated sugar

2 tbsp soft light brown sugar

2 tbsp plain flour, plus extra for dusting

½ tsp ground cinnamon

⅛ tsp ground nutmeg

1. Preheat the oven to 220°C/425°F/Gas Mark 7.

2. Divide the pastry into two pieces, roll out one piece on a lightly floured work surface and cut out six 7.5-cm/3-inch rounds. Place one round in the base of each of six 225-ml/8-fl oz wide-mouthed preserving jars. Press the pastry into the base and up the sides a little.

3. Put the apples and lemon juice into a large bowl and mix together, then add the granulated sugar, brown sugar, flour, cinnamon and nutmeg and toss to coat the apples. Divide the mixture between the jars, packing it in as tightly as you can.

4. Roll out the remaining dough on a lightly floured work surface and cut out six 7.5-cm/3-inch rounds. Use a fork to pierce several small holes in each round, then place 1 round on top of the filling in each jar, tucking the edges inside the rims of the jars. Use the tines of a fork to create a decorative edge on the pastry, or use your fingers to fold and pleat it into a decorative border. Place the jars on a Swiss roll tin and bake in the preheated oven for about 15 minutes, then reduce the heat to 190°C/375°F/Gas Mark 5 and bake for a further 30–35 minutes, until the filling is bubbling and the pastry is golden brown and crisp. Remove from the oven and leave to cool for 10–15 minutes. Serve warm.

2.

3.

4.

★ Cook's Tips ★

Prepare the cobbler up to the point of sprinkling the sugar,
seal the jars with their lids and store in the freezer for up to 3
months. To serve, preheat the oven to 180°C/350°F/Gas Mark 4,
remove the lids and bake in the preheated oven for 40 minutes,
until cooked through.

This pretty and sweet mixed berry treat is a great way to enjoy summer's bounty year-round.

Berry Cobblers

MAKES: 8 small jars

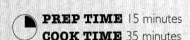

PREP TIME 15 minutes
COOK TIME 35 minutes

INGREDIENTS:

575 g/1 lb 4½ oz mixed berries (any combination of blackberries, raspberries, blueberries and strawberries), thawed and drained, if frozen

100 g/3½ oz sugar

1 tbsp lemon juice

2 tbsp cornflour

Topping

125 g/4½ oz plain flour

25 g/1 oz granulated sugar

½ tsp cinnamon

pinch of salt

60 g/2¼ oz unsalted butter

4 tbsp double cream

1 large egg

4 tsp soft dark brown sugar

1. Preheat the oven to 180°C/350°F/Gas Mark 4.

2. Put the berries, sugar, lemon juice and cornflour into a medium-sized bowl and mix to combine. Divide the mixture between eight 225-ml/8-fl oz wide-mouthed preserving jars.

3. To make the topping, put the flour, sugar, cinnamon and salt into a food processor and pulse to combine. Add the butter and pulse until the mixture resembles coarse crumbs. Add the cream and egg and process until the mixture comes together into a loose, sticky ball.

4. Spoon the topping onto the berry mixture, dividing it between the jars. Sprinkle the brown sugar over the tops and bake in the preheated oven for about 35 minutes, until the topping is golden brown and cooked through. Serve warm.

★ Cook's Tips ★

Prepare the macaroni cheese up to the point of adding the
breadcrumb topping. Seal the jars with their lids and freeze
for up to 3 months. To serve, preheat the oven to 190°C/375°F/
Gas Mark 5. Remove the lids and bake them in the preheated
oven for 30 minutes until cooked through.

Bubbling away in see-through jars, this rich, creamy pasta dish with its crunchy breadcrumb topping is irresistible.

Macaroni Cheese

MAKES: 8 small jars or 4 large jars

 PREP TIME 15 minutes
COOK TIME 35 minutes

INGREDIENTS:

oil, for greasing

450 g/1 lb dried elbow macaroni

115 g/4 oz unsalted butter

2 tbsp plain flour

300 ml/10 fl oz light cream

350 g/12 oz mature Gouda, Cheddar or Gruyère cheese, coarsely grated

125 g/4½ oz fontina cheese, coarsely grated

2 tsp sweet or smoked paprika

½ tsp salt

½ tsp pepper

Topping

45 g/1⅓ oz panko breadcrumbs

3 tbsp unsalted butter, melted

25 g/1 oz freshly grated Parmesan cheese

1. Preheat the oven to 190°C/375°F/Gas Mark 5 and grease eight 225-ml/8-fl oz or four 475-ml/16-fl oz wide-mouthed preserving jars and place them on a Swiss roll tin.

2. Cook the pasta according to the packet instructions until tender, but still firm to the bite. Drain, reserving 125 ml/4 fl oz of the cooking water.

3. Melt the butter in a large saucepan. Add the flour and whisk over a medium heat until the mixture is just beginning to brown and is giving off a nutty aroma. Reduce the heat to low and stir in the cream until fully incorporated. Remove the pan from the heat and stir in the Gouda cheese and fontina cheese until completely melted. If the sauce is too thick, add a little of the reserved pasta cooking water, 1 tablespoon at a time, stirring until incorporated. Add more water if needed to achieve the desired consistency. Stir in the paprika, salt and pepper. Add the pasta and stir to coat well. Divide the pasta between the jars.

4. To make the topping, combine the breadcrumbs, melted butter and Parmesan cheese. Spoon over the top of the pasta, dividing equally.

5. Bake the jars in the preheated oven for about 25 minutes, until the mixture is bubbling and the topping is golden brown. Leave to stand for 1–2 minutes before serving.

Focaccia is ideally suited for cooking in single-serving portions with a crisp golden crust all around and a pillowy interior.

Olive, Sun-Dried Tomato & Sage Focaccia

MAKES: 12 small jars

PREP TIME 15 minutes, plus 2 hours 15 minutes to rise
COOK TIME 35 minutes

INGREDIENTS:

400 ml/14 fl oz lukewarm water

7 g/⅛ oz easy-blend dried yeast

1 tbsp sugar

600 g/1 lb 5 oz strong white flour, plus extra if needed and for dusting

1 tbsp salt

225 ml/8 fl oz olive oil, plus extra for oiling and drizzling

60 g/2¼ oz Kalamata olives, chopped

25 g/1 oz sun-dried tomatoes, chopped

1 tbsp chopped fresh sage

coarse salt, for sprinkling

1. Put the water into a large mixing bowl and sprinkle over the yeast and sugar. Leave to stand in a warm place for 15–20 minutes, or until the mixture is foaming.

2. Add the flour, salt and half the oil to the yeast mixture and mix with an electric mixer on low speed until the dough begins to come together. Knead the dough for about 5 minutes, until it is smooth and springy. The dough should be fairly wet and sticky, but if it is too wet to handle, add more flour, 1 tablespoon at a time, until the desired consistency is achieved.

3. Turn out the dough onto a lightly floured board and knead in the olives, tomatoes and sage until thoroughly combined. Form the dough into a ball and put it into a large, oiled bowl. Turn the ball until it is coated with oil. Loosely cover with a clean tea towel and leave to stand in a warm place for about 1 hour, or until doubled in size.

4. Place 1 teaspoon of the remaining oil in each of twelve 225-ml/8-fl oz wide-mouthed preserving jars, turning the jars so that the insides are completely coated. Divide the dough into 12 balls and place 1 ball in each of the prepared jars. Turn the balls in the jars until they are coated with oil. Place the jars on a Swiss roll tin and set aside for about 1 hour, or until doubled in size.

5. Meanwhile, preheat the oven to 220°C/425°F/Gas Mark 7. Drizzle the dough balls with a little oil and sprinkle with coarse salt. Bake in the preheated oven for about 35 minutes, until the tops are puffed and golden brown. Serve the focaccia warm or at room temperature.

★ Cook's Tips ★

The focaccia can be covered with foil and stored at room temperature for 1-2 days. To keep for longer, remove from the jars, place in polythene freezer bags and freeze for up to 3 months. Bring to room temperature before serving.

Children and adults alike will be delighted by these individual pizzas made with a simple tomato sauce, creamy fresh mozzarella and fresh basil.

Pizza Margherita

MAKES: 12 small jars

 PREP TIME 45 minutes, plus 1¼ hours to rise
COOK TIME 50 minutes

INGREDIENTS:

400 ml/14 fl oz lukewarm water

7 g/⅝ oz easy-blend dried yeast

1 tbsp sugar

600 g/1 lb 5 oz strong white flour, plus extra for dusting

1 tbsp salt

125 ml/4 fl oz olive oil, plus extra for oiling and drizzling

450 g/1 lb fresh mozzarella cheese, thinly sliced

handful of fresh basil, shredded

coarse salt, for sprinkling

Sauce

1 tbsp unsalted butter

1 tbsp olive oil

2 garlic cloves, finely chopped

2 shallots, diced

800 g/1 lb 12 oz canned San Marzano tomatoes, diced, with their can juices

¼ tsp chilli flakes

salt and pepper

1. Put the water into a large mixing bowl and sprinkle over the yeast and sugar. Leave to stand in a warm place for 15–20 minutes, or until the mixture is foaming.

2. Add the flour, salt and half the oil to the yeast mixture and mix with an electric mixer on low speed until the dough begins to come together. Knead the dough for about 5 minutes, until it is smooth and springy. The dough should be fairly wet and sticky, but if it is too wet to handle, add more flour, 1 tablespoon at a time, until the desired consistency is achieved.

3. Turn out the dough onto a lightly floured board and knead for 1–2 minutes, dusting with a little flour if needed. Form the dough into a ball and put it into a large, oiled bowl. Turn the ball until it is coated with oil. Loosely cover with a clean tea towel and leave to stand in a warm place for about 1 hour, or until doubled in size.

4. Meanwhile, make the sauce. Heat the butter and oil in a medium-sized saucepan until the butter is melted and the oil is hot. Add the garlic and shallots and cook, stirring, for about 4 minutes until soft. Add the tomatoes, ½ teaspoon of salt, ½ teaspoon of pepper and the chilli flakes and bring to the boil. Reduce the heat to medium–low and simmer for about 45 minutes, or until thick. Using a handheld blender or food processor, purée the sauce until smooth. Add salt and pepper to taste.

5. Oil twelve 225-ml/8 fl oz wide-mouthed preserving jars and place them on a Swiss roll tin. Preheat the oven to 200°C/400°F/Gas Mark 6.

6. Divide the dough into 2 pieces. Return 1 piece to the bowl and cover with the tea towel. Divide the other piece into 12 balls. Roll out or press each ball into a 10-cm/4-inch round and place 1 round in the base of each of the prepared jars, pressing it into the base and up the sides. Bake in the preheated oven for about 20–25 minutes, until the crusts are light brown and crisp.

To store, leave to cool to room temperature, then seal the jars with their lids. Store in the refrigerator for 2-3 days or in the freezer for up to 3 months. To serve, preheat the oven to 180°C/350°F/Gas Mark 4. Remove the lids from the jars and cook for about 20 minutes. Serve hot.

---

7. Make twelve more rounds with the remaining dough. Remove the jars from the oven (do not switch off the oven) and spoon sauce into each on top of the pizza bases, filling each jar with 4–5 cm/1½–2 inches of sauce. Top the sauce with the mozzarella cheese and the basil. Top with another pizza base round, pushing it down into the jar. Drizzle a little oil over the top and sprinkle with coarse salt. Return to the oven and bake for about 25–30 minutes, until the top is brown and crisp. Serve hot.

3.

4.

7.

★ Cook's Tips ★

The tarts can be stored in the freezer, unbaked, for up to 3 months. Assemble the tart with the uncooked pastry. Seal the jars with their lids and store in the freezer. To serve, remove the lids, preheat the oven to 220°C/425°F/Gas Mark 7 and bake for 20–25 minutes, or until cooked through.

Layers of golden pastry conceal a rich, tangy goat's cheese custard studded with succulent asparagus.

Asparagus Tarts

MAKES: 8 small jars

PREP TIME 15 minutes
COOK TIME 30 minutes

INGREDIENTS:

400 g/14 oz ready-made shortcrust pastry

flour, for dusting

450 g/1 lb asparagus, cut into 2.5-cm/1-inch pieces

90 ml/3 fl oz water

4 eggs

115 g/4 oz goat's cheese

325 ml/11 fl oz light cream

¾ tsp salt

½ tsp pepper

zest of 1 lemon

1. Preheat the oven to 220°C/425°F/Gas Mark 7.

2. Divide the pastry into two pieces, roll out one piece on a lightly floured work surface and cut out eight 7.5-cm/3-inch rounds. Place one round in the base of each of eight 225-ml/8-fl oz wide-mouthed preserving jars. Use a fork to pierce several holes in each round. Place the jars on a Swiss roll tin and bake in the preheated oven for about 15 minutes, until the pastry is light brown. Remove from the oven, but do not switch off the oven.

3. Meanwhile, put the asparagus into a medium-sized microwaveable bowl with the water. Cover with clingfilm and heat on High for 1–2 minutes until just tender.

4. Put the eggs, cheese, cream, salt, pepper and lemon zest into a bowl and beat with an electric mixer until smooth. Divide the mixture between the jars, ladling it over the pastry. Divide the asparagus between the jars, arranging it on the custard in a single layer.

5. Roll out the remaining pastry and cut out eight 7.5-cm/3-inch rounds. Use a fork to pierce several holes in each round, then place one round on top of the filling in each jar, tucking the edges inside the rims of the jars. Bake in the preheated oven for about 15 minutes, until the filling is set and the pastry lid is golden brown and crisp. Leave to cool for a few minutes, then serve.

2.

4.

4.

33

MAKE

Make

As the photos on these pages show, canning jars make wonderfully attractive serving vessels and lend a fashionable air of retro-chic to a party table. Fill them with layers of colourful foods – from rainbow-coloured salads to layered desserts – for a stunning presentation that will be a talking point among your guests. Better still, filled jars can be lidded and taken along for a picnic, car or train journey, cake sale, a day at the office or any other time you want to take your meal with you.

For best results, give some thought to how your jars will look before you begin filling them and think, also, about how the ingredients will interact with each other in the jar. For instance, when making salads, dressing should always go in first with sturdy ingredients going in just on top of the dressing and more delicate ingredients, such as salad leaves, at the top of the jar. This way, the dressing won't make the lettuce soggy and your salad will remain fresh and crisp in the refrigerator. Just before serving, with the lid still on, you can shake your jar of salad to distribute the dressing throughout. *Voilà*! Tossed salad in an instant.

Think, too, about how your ingredients will look when layered in the jar. Put contrasting colours and textures next to each other for the greatest visual impact. Layer ingredients neatly and shake or tap the jars to even out the layers as you go. To keep the layers, and the jar rims, neat, use a wide-mouthed funnel, an ice-cream scoop, a ladle or even a piping bag to fill the jars.

Red Velvet Cakes

The rich red hue of this chocolatey cake is set off beautifully against layers of snow-white buttercream.

MAKES: 6 small jars

PREP TIME 20 minutes
COOK TIME 20 minutes

INGREDIENTS:

200 g/7 oz plain flour

3 tbsp cocoa powder

¼ tsp salt

115 g/4 oz unsalted butter, at room temperature, plus extra for greasing

300 g/10½ oz caster sugar

1 tsp vanilla extract

2 large eggs

150 ml/5 fl oz buttermilk

1 tbsp red gel food colouring

1 tsp cider vinegar

1 tsp bicarbonate of soda

chocolate shavings, mini chocolate chips or chocolate vermicelli, to decorate

Frosting
3 egg whites

150 g/5½ oz sugar

225 g/8 oz unsalted butter, at room temperature

1 tbsp vanilla extract

1. Preheat the oven to 180°C/350°F/Gas Mark 4 and grease a 23 x 33-cm/9 x 13-inch cake tin.

2. Put the flour, cocoa powder and salt into a medium-sized bowl and mix to combine.

3. Put the butter and sugar into a large bowl and beat with an electric mixer set on high speed, until pale and fluffy. Add the vanilla extract, then add the eggs, one at a time, beating after each addition until incorporated. Add half the flour mixture and beat on medium speed until incorporated. Scrape down the side of the bowl, add the buttermilk and food colouring and beat until incorporated. Scrape down the side of the bowl, add the remaining flour mixture and beat until just incorporated. Put the vinegar and bicarbonate of soda into a small bowl and stir to combine. Add to the batter and beat until incorporated.

4. Transfer the batter to the prepared tin, smoothing the top with a spatula. Bake in the preheated oven for about 20 minutes, until a cocktail stick inserted into the centre comes out clean. Remove from the oven and leave to cool for several minutes, then turn out onto a wire rack to cool completely.

5. To make the frosting, heat some water in the base of a double boiler until just simmering. Put the egg whites and sugar into the top of the double boiler and mix to combine. Set over the simmering water (the pan should be touching the water) and whisk constantly for about 5 minutes, until the sugar is completely dissolved (dip in a thumb and finger and rub together; if there are no grains left, the sugar is fully dissolved) and the mixture is warm. Remove from the heat and, using an electric mixer fitted with a whisk attachment, beat the mixture on high speed for about 5 minutes, until it holds stiff, glossy peaks. Add the butter, 1–2 tablespoons at a time, and beat until the mixture holds stiff peaks. Add the vanilla extract and beat until just combined.

★ Cook's Tips ★

The finished cakes can be stored in the lidded jars in the refrigerator for up to 2 days or in the freezer for up to 3 months. Bring to room temperature before serving.

6. Using a 6-cm/2½-inch round cutter, cut out twelve rounds out of the cake. Place one round in the base of each of six 225-ml/8-fl oz wide-mouthed preserving jars. Top each cake round with a large spoonful of the frosting and then a second round of cake. Finish with another large spoonful of frosting, smoothing the top with the back of the spoon. Sprinkle with chocolate shavings and serve immediately.

Rich devil's food cake, creamy peanut butter frosting and a dark chocolate shell combine to make one irresistible dessert.

Chocolate Peanut Butter Cupcakes

MAKES: 6 large jars or 12 small jars

PREP TIME 30 minutes
COOK TIME 20 minutes

INGREDIENTS:

125 g/4½ oz plain flour

65 g/2¾ oz cocoa powder

1½ tsp baking powder

¼ tsp salt

115 g/4 oz unsalted butter, at room temperature, plus extra for greasing

200 g/7 oz caster sugar

2 tsp vanilla extract

2 large eggs

125 ml/4 fl oz double cream

Frosting & topping

115 g/4 oz unsalted butter, softened

125 g/4½ oz smooth peanut butter

185–315 g/6½–10¾ oz icing sugar

2 tbsp milk

pinch of salt

225 g/8 oz plain chocolate coating

2 tbsp vegetable oil

1. Preheat the oven to 180°C/350°/Gas Mark 4 and grease a 23 × 33-cm/9 × 13-inch cake tin.

2. To make the cake, put the flour, cocoa powder, baking powder and salt into a medium-sized bowl.

3. Put the butter and sugar into a large bowl and beat with an electric mixer set on high speed for several minutes, until pale yellow and fluffy. Add the vanilla extract, then add the eggs, one at a time, beating after each addition until incorporated. Add half the flour mixture and beat on medium speed until incorporated. Scrape down the side of the bowl, add the cream, and beat until incorporated. Scrape down the side of the bowl, add the remaining flour mixture and beat until just incorporated.

4. Spoon the batter into the prepared tin, smoothing the top. Bake in the preheated oven for about 20 minutes, until a cocktail stick inserted into the centre comes out clean. Leave to cool in the tin for 1–2 minutes, then transfer to a wire rack to cool completely.

5. To make the frosting, put the butter and peanut butter into a medium-sized bowl and beat with an electric mixer until creamy. Add 185 g/6½ oz of the icing sugar, the milk and salt. Beat together until well combined. Gradually beat in more icing sugar, until the desired consistency is achieved.

6. Place the cake on a flat surface and use a 6-cm/2½-inch round cutter to cut out 12 rounds.

7. If making 475-ml/16-fl oz jars, place one round of cake in the base of each of six wide-mouthed jars. Spoon 2–3 tablespoons of frosting on top, smoothing with the back of a spoon. Top the frosting with a second layer of cake and top that with a second layer of frosting, smoothing the top.

8. If making twelve 225-ml/8-fl oz jars, layer them with 1 round of cake and 1 layer of frosting.

4.

5.

7.

9. To make the topping, put the chocolate coating and oil into a small microwaveable bowl and heat on Low for 30 seconds at a time, until the chocolate is mostly melted. Stir vigorously with a fork until the chocolate is completely melted.

10. Spoon the chocolate over the tops of the frosted cakes so that the frosting is completely covered in chocolate. Chill in the refrigerator for 5–10 minutes, until the chocolate is set. Serve at room temperature.

★ Cook's Tips ★

Refrigerate the cakes in the covered jars for up to
3 days or freeze them for up to 3 months. Bring
to room temperature before serving.

★ Cook's Tips ★

The panna cottas will keep, covered, in the refrigerator
for several days. The compote can be added to the panna cottas once
they have set or just before serving.

This light and refreshing milk pudding is as delicious as it is beautiful. Any type of berry – strawberries, blueberries, raspberries or a combination – will work just as well for the compote.

Orange Panna Cotta

MAKES: 6 small jars

 PREP TIME 15 minutes, plus at least 4 hours to chill
COOK TIME 10 minutes

INGREDIENTS:

3 tbsp freshly squeezed orange juice

2¼ tsp gelatine

1 litre/1¾ pints milk

100 g/3½ oz sugar

1 tsp vanilla extract

2 tsp grated orange zest

Blackberry compote

225 g/8 oz fresh or frozen blackberries

4 tbsp water

50 g/1¾ oz sugar

2 tbsp lemon juice

1. Put the orange juice into a small bowl and sprinkle over the gelatine. Set aside until the gelatine has absorbed the liquid.

2. Put the milk, sugar and vanilla extract into a medium-sized saucepan over a medium–high heat, and bring to simmering point, stirring to incorporate the sugar. Remove from the heat and stir in the orange zest and the gelatine mixture. Whisk until the gelatine is fully dissolved. Divide the mixture between six 225-ml/8-fl oz wide-mouthed preserving jars. Leave to cool to room temperature, then seal the jars with their lids and refrigerate for at least 4 hours until set.

3. To make the compote, put the ingredients into a medium-sized saucepan over a medium-high heat and stir to combine. Bring to the boil, then reduce the heat to medium–low and simmer until the sugar is dissolved, the liquid is beginning to thicken and the fruit is beginning to break down. Remove from the heat and leave to cool to room temperature.

4. Remove the lids from the jars of panna cotta, spoon the compote over the tops and serve immediately.

Refrigerator cakes are perfect for single-serving preserving jars.

Gingersnap Refrigerator Cakes

MAKES: 6 small jars

PREP TIME 15 minutes, plus 4 hours to chill
COOK TIME No cooking

INGREDIENTS:

475 ml/16 fl oz double cream

50 g/1¾ oz sugar

zest and juice of 1 lemon

36 gingersnaps, 12 broken in half

40 g/1½ oz chopped crystallized ginger, to decorate

1. Put the cream into a large bowl and whip until it holds stiff peaks. Add the sugar and the lemon zest and juice and beat until combined.

2. Spoon about 2 tablespoons of the mixture into the base of each of six 225-ml/8-fl oz wide-mouthed preserving jars. Top each cream layer with 1½ biscuits in a single layer.

3. Spoon another 2 tablespoons of the cream mixture on top of the biscuits, and top with another 1½ biscuits. Repeat until there are 4 layers of biscuits.

4. Finish with a layer of cream. Wipe the rims of the jars clean and seal the jars with their lids. Chill in the refrigerator for at least 4 hours.

5. Just before serving, remove the lids and sprinkle the ginger over the tops.

 **1.**

 **2.**

 **4.**

★ Cook's Tips ★

The cakes will keep in the refrigerator for up to 3 days or in
the freezer for up to 3 months. Remove the frozen cakes from
the freezer and refrigerate for at least 4 hours before serving.
Sprinkle over the ginger just before serving.

★ Cook's Tips ★

Banana splits can be frozen for up to 3 months. Follow the
recipe up to the addition of the third layer of ice cream. Seal
the jars with their lids and freeze. Remove from the freezer
about 10 minutes before serving. Add the chocolate sauce,
whipped cream, nuts and cherries just before serving.

Banana Splits

Three flavours of ice cream alternate with layers of sliced bananas under a drizzle of rich chocolate sauce. Whipped cream, nuts and a cherry on top are the perfect finish.

MAKES: 6 large jars

⏱ **PREP TIME** 15 minutes
COOK TIME 5 minutes

INGREDIENTS:

450 g/1 lb chocolate ice cream

450 g/1 lb vanilla ice cream

450 g/1 lb strawberry ice cream

6 ripe bananas, sliced

Chocolate sauce

115 g/4 oz plain chocolate, chopped

125 ml/4 fl oz double cream

2 tbsp unsalted butter, diced

pinch of salt

To decorate

225 ml/8 fl oz whipped cream

3 tbsp chopped nuts

6 maraschino cherries

1. Remove the ice cream from the freezer and leave to soften for about 10 minutes.

2. Meanwhile, to make the chocolate sauce, put the chocolate, cream, butter and salt into a microwaveable glass measuring jug. Heat on Low for 30 seconds at a time until the cream is hot and the chocolate is mostly melted. Stir vigorously until the chocolate is completely melted and is well incorporated with the other ingredients. Leave to cool for a few minutes.

3. Place one third of the slices from 1 banana in the base of each of six 225-ml/8-fl oz wide-mouthed preserving jars. Put a scoop of strawberry ice cream into each jar, flattening it with the back of the spoon. Add a second layer of banana slices and top with a scoop of chocolate ice cream. Top with a third layer of banana slices, then add a scoop of vanilla ice cream. Drizzle chocolate sauce over the top, allowing it to drip down the sides. Top each jar with whipped cream, a sprinkling of nuts and a maraschino cherry and serve immediately.

2.

3.

3.

The simple syrup will keep indefinitely, stored in a lidded jar in the refrigerator. This recipe can easily make smaller cocktails. Use twelve 225-ml/8-fl oz jars and halve the quantity of each of the ingredients for the individual cocktails.

Don't get stuck playing bartender at your next barbecue. Mix up cocktails in mason jars and stash them in a bucket of ice so that guests can help themselves.

Mojitos to Go

MAKES: 6 large jars

PREP TIME 10 minutes
COOK TIME 5 minutes

INGREDIENTS:

30 fresh mint leaves, plus extra to serve

1.7 litres/3 pints soda water

350–500 ml/12–18 fl oz light rum

225 ml/8 fl oz lime juice

ice cubes, and lime wedges, to serve

Mint simple syrup
300 g/10½ oz sugar

350 ml/12 fl oz water

20 g/¾ oz fresh mint leaves, torn into pieces

1. To prepare the simple syrup, put the sugar and water into a saucepan set over a medium–high heat and bring to the boil. Reduce the heat to medium and cook, stirring, for about 2 minutes until the sugar is completely dissolved. Remove from the heat, stir in the mint leaves, cover and leave to steep for about 1 hour. Strain the syrup into a jar, discarding the mint leaves, and store, covered, in the refrigerator until ready to use.

2. To make the cocktails, put 85 ml/3 fl oz simple syrup in each of the six 475-m/16-fl oz mason jars. Add 5 fresh mint leaves to each jar, crinkling them with your fingers before you add them. Muddle together the mint and simple syrup using the back of a spoon or a cocktail muddler. Add 300 ml/10 fl oz soda water, 50–85 ml/2–3 fl oz rum and 3 tablespoons of lime juice to each jar. Seal the jars with their lids and shake very gently to mix. Store the jars in the refrigerator, cool box or a bucket of ice until ready to serve. Serve cold, decorated with fresh mint sprigs, ice cubes and lime wedges.

1.

2.

2.

Roasted Beetroot & Rocket Salad

Deep red beetroot at the bottom, bright candied orange zest at the top, and fresh green rocket in the middle make for a beautifully refreshing salad.

MAKES: 6 large jars

PREP TIME 15 minutes
COOK TIME 2 hours 40 minutes, plus overnight to crisp the orange zest

INGREDIENTS:

Candied Orange Zest

2 large navel oranges

100 g/3½ oz sugar

Vinaigrette

4 tbsp white wine vinegar

2 tbsp Dijon mustard

2 tsp honey

1 tsp salt

½ tsp pepper

4 tbsp olive oil

Salad

6 beetroot

6 handfuls rocket

85 g/3 oz blue cheese, crumbled

25 g/1 oz walnuts or pecan nuts

1. To make the candied orange zest, use a vegetable peeler to remove the zest from the oranges, leaving all the white pith behind. Cut the zest into 5-mm/¼-inch wide strips. Put them into a small saucepan, cover with cold water and bring to the boil over a medium–high heat. Reduce the heat to medium and simmer for 5 minutes. Remove from the heat and drain in a colander.

2. Put the sugar into the pan with 125 ml/4 fl oz water and heat over a medium heat until the sugar is completely dissolved. Add the drained zest to the pan and bring to simmering point. Reduce the heat to low and simmer gently for about 20 minutes, until the zest is translucent.

3. Meanwhile, preheat the oven to its lowest setting and line a baking sheet with baking paper.

4. Remove the zest from the pan using a slotted spoon, allowing the excess liquid to drain off. Spread the zest on the prepared baking sheet in a single layer and place in the preheated oven for 1 hour. Switch off the oven, but do not remove the zest. Leave it in the oven overnight, or for up to 24 hours, until it is crisp.

5. To make the salad, preheat the oven to 240°C/475°F/Gas Mark 9.

6. Wrap each beetroot in foil and bake in the preheated oven for about 1 hour 15 minutes, until tender. Remove from the oven and leave to cool. When cool enough to handle, slip off the skins and dice the beetroot.

7. To make the vinaigrette, combine the vinegar, mustard, honey, salt and pepper in a small bowl and whisk to combine. Add the oil and whisk until emulsified.

8. Toss half the dressing with the beetroot and toss the remainder with the rocket. Divide the beetroot between six 475-ml/16-fl oz wide-mouthed preserving jars. Add the dressed rocket, then a layer of cheese and a layer of nuts. Garnish each jar with a sprinkling of candied orange zest and serve immediately.

1.   7.   8.

★ Cook's Tips ★

The salads can be stored in the refrigerator for up to 3 days. To make them ahead, divide all the dressing between the jars, then layer in the beetroot, rocket, cheese, nuts and zest. Seal the jars with their lids and refrigerate for up to 3 days. Shake before serving to distribute the dressing.

★ Cook's Tips ★

These salads can be made up to 3 days ahead.
Seal the finished salads with their lids and store
in the refrigerator. Bring to room temperature
before serving.

Preserving jars are the perfect way to show off the bright, fresh colours of this hearty salad.

Quinoa Salads

MAKES: 12 small jars or 6 large jars

◑ **PREP TIME** 15 minutes
COOK TIME 15 minutes

INGREDIENTS:

250 g/9 oz red or golden quinoa

4 spring onions, thinly sliced

325 g/11½ oz fresh strawberries, sliced

115 g/4 oz fresh goat's cheese, crumbled

85 g/3 oz roasted unsalted pistachio nuts, chopped

handful of fresh mint leaves, chopped

Dressing

90 ml/3 fl oz lemon juice

1 tsp honey

1 tsp Dijon mustard

½ tsp salt

½ tsp pepper

150 ml/5 fl oz olive oil

1. Cook the quinoa according to the packet instructions and leave to cool.

2. To make the dressing, combine the lemon juice, honey, mustard, salt and pepper in a small jar or bowl and shake or whisk to combine. Add the oil and shake or whisk vigorously until emulsified.

3. Toss 3 tablespoons of the dressing with the cooked quinoa.

4. To compose the salads, place 1 tablespoon of the dressing in each of twelve 225-ml/8-fl oz wide-mouthed preserving jars, or place 2 tablespoons of the dressing in each of six 475-ml/16-fl oz jars. Add a layer of quinoa to each jar. Sprinkle over the spring onions, add a layer of strawberries, a layer of cheese and a layer of nuts, then top with mint. Spoon a little more dressing over the top and serve immediately.

1.

4.

4.

TAKE

Take

With the DIY trend going strong at the moment, home-made gifts are more fashionable than they've ever been. And what could be better than a home-made gift of something delicious? Preserving jars are ideal gift packaging for ready-to-bake cookies or easy-to-finish mixes for soup, pretzels, brownies, muffins, pancakes and much, much more.

For great food gifts in jars, use clean, unchipped jars with lids that seal tightly. Be sure to include storage instructions, which can be found in the Cook's Tips section of each recipe, as well as information for how to bake or make the final product (also included with each recipe). Dry mixes will keep indefinitely in a cool, dark place and ready-to-bake cookie dough can be frozen.

Filling the jars is only half the fun. Get creative with pretty gift tags, labels, cooking instructions and ribbons. Cover the tops with decorative paper or squares of colourful cloth. Your food gifts will be as beautiful as they are appetizing.

And just think how the recipients will delight in the gift when they first receive it, then rejoice once more when their house is filled with the smell of hot lentil soup, or fresh-baked pretzels, brownies or cookies.

Chocolate Chip Coconut Cookies

The classic chocolate chip cookie gets a makeover. Sweet desiccated coconut adds an addictive chewiness, while puffed rice cereal gives some unexpected crunch.

MAKES: 6 large jars, each with 12 cookies

 PREP TIME 20 minutes, plus at least 4 hours to freeze
COOK TIME No cooking

INGREDIENTS:

250 g/9 oz plain flour

1½ tsp bicarbonate of soda

¾ tsp salt

170 g/5¾ oz unsalted butter, at room temperature

150 g/5½ oz soft light brown sugar

150 g/5½ oz granulated sugar

1 tbsp vanilla extract

2 large eggs

150 g/5½ oz puffed rice cereal

150 g/5½ oz sweetened desiccated coconut

260 g/9½ oz mini plain chocolate chips

1. Line two large baking sheets with baking paper. Put the flour, bicarbonate of soda and salt into a medium-sized bowl and mix to combine.

2. Put the butter, brown sugar and granulated sugar into a large bowl and beat with an electric mixer until pale and fluffy. Scrape down the side of the bowl, add the vanilla extract, then add the eggs and beat until incorporated. Add the flour mixture and beat until well combined. Stir in the rice cereal, coconut and chocolate chips.

3. Use your hands to form the dough into 2.5-cm/1-inch balls and place them on the prepared baking sheets. You should have 72 dough balls. Place the sheets in the freezer for at least 4 hours or overnight, until the balls are completely frozen.

4. Place 12 frozen dough balls in each of six 475-ml/16-fl oz wide-mouthed preserving jars. Attach a gift tag to each jar with these instructions:

How to bake Chocolate Chip Coconut Cookies

Keep frozen until required. Preheat the oven to 180°C/350°F/Gas Mark 4 and place the frozen dough balls on an ungreased baking sheet, spaced about 5 cm/2 inches apart. Bake in the preheated oven for about 12 minutes, until the cookies have spread out and are beginning to brown around the edges. Remove from the oven and leave to cool on the sheet for 1–2 minutes. Using a spatula, transfer the cookies to a wire rack to cool. Serve warm or at room temperature.

2.

2.

3.

★ Cook's Tips ★

The frozen dough will keep in the freezer, tightly
sealed, for up to 3 months.

61

1.

2.

3.

★ Cook's Tips ★

The cookies will keep in the freezer, tightly sealed,
for up to 3 months.

These spicy ginger thins will not only tickle your recipients' tongues, but will fill their homes with the festive aroma of freshly baked cookies.

Christmas Ginger Thins

MAKES: 6 large jars, each with 12 cookies

PREP TIME 30 minutes, plus at least 4 hours to freeze
COOK TIME No cooking

INGREDIENTS:

500 g/1 lb 2 oz plain flour

2 tsp bicarbonate of soda

1 tsp salt

2 tbsp ground ginger

2 tsp ground cinnamon

1 tsp ground cloves

345 g/11¾ oz unsalted butter, at room temperature

200 g/7 oz granulated sugar

200 g/7 oz soft dark brown sugar

2 large eggs

245 g/8¾ oz treacle

400 g/14 oz coarse brown sugar

1. Line two large baking sheets with baking paper.

2. Put the flour, bicarbonate of soda, salt, ginger, cinnamon and cloves into a medium-sized bowl and mix to combine.

3. Put the butter, granulated sugar and soft dark brown sugar into a large bowl and beat with an electric mixer until light and fluffy. Add the eggs and treacle and mix until incorporated. Add the flour mixture and beat until incorporated, scraping down the side of the bowl once or twice.

4. Put the coarse brown sugar in a shallow bowl. Shape the dough into 4-cm/1½-inch balls and roll in the sugar to coat completely. Place the balls on the prepared baking sheet spaced well apart. When the first sheet is full, use your fingertips to flatten the balls into rounds about 7.5 cm/3 inches in diameter (they should be about the same diameter as the preserving jars) and 2.5 mm/⅛ inch thick. If your fingers become too sticky, dip them in the sugar. Place the sheet in the freezer. Continue to shape the remaining dough until all the dough has been used and both sheets are full. Place the second sheet in the freezer and freeze for at least 4 hours or overnight, until the cookies are completely frozen.

5. Stack 12 frozen cookies in each of six 475-ml/16-fl oz wide-mouthed preserving jars. Attach a gift tag to each jar with these instructions:

How to bake Christmas Ginger Thins

Keep frozen until required. Preheat the oven to 180°C/350°F/Gas Mark 4 and place the cookies on an ungreased baking sheet. Bake in the preheated oven for 12–14 minutes, until the cookies are dry on the top and beginning to crisp. Remove from the oven and transfer to a wire rack to cool. Serve at room temperature.

**These decadent brownies beat a
packet brownie mix any day.**

Double Chocolate Brownie Mix

**MAKES: 6 large jars, each
with sufficient mix
for 12 brownies**

PREP TIME 10 minutes
COOK TIME No cooking

INGREDIENTS:

750 g/1 lb 10 oz plain flour

1½ tsp salt

600 g/1 lb 5 oz soft light
brown sugar

800 g/1 lb 12 oz granulated sugar

350 g/12 oz cocoa powder

450 g/1 lb toasted hazelnuts,
chopped

525 g/1 lb 3 oz mini plain chocolate
chips

1. To prepare the gift jars, divide all of the ingredients evenly between six 475-ml/16-fl oz wide-mouthed preserving jars. Add the ingredients in layers, starting with the flour. Place the lids on the jars and secure tightly.

2. Attach a gift tag to each jar with these instructions:

How to prepare Double Chocolate Brownies

You will need:

2 large eggs

2 tbsp milk

1 tsp vanilla extract

115 g/4 oz butter, melted, plus extra for greasing

Preheat the oven to 180°C/350°F/Gas Mark 4 and grease a 23 × 33-cm/9 × 13-inch rectangular cake tin.

Transfer the brownie mix from the jar to a large mixing bowl. Put the eggs, milk and vanilla extract into a separate bowl and mix to combine. Add the egg mixture to the dry ingredients and mix until well combined. Stir in the melted butter and mix to combine.

Transfer the batter to the prepared tin and bake in the preheated oven for about 20 minutes, until the top is dry and a cocktail stick inserted into the centre comes out almost clean. Place the tin on a wire rack and leave to cool completely. Serve at room temperature.

1.   1.   1.

★ Cook's Tips ★

The brownie mix will keep for up to 6 months.
Cover tightly and store in a cool, dry place.

With just a few staples, this mix transforms into a delicious, nutritious breakfast treat.

Cherry-almond Muffin Mix

MAKES: 6 large jars, each with sufficient mix for 6 muffins

PREP TIME 10 minutes
COOK TIME No cooking

INGREDIENTS:

300 g/10½ oz soft light brown sugar

425 g/15 oz dried cherries

300 g/10½ oz granulated sugar

140 g/5 oz ground almonds

4½ tsp baking powder

1½ tsp salt

550 g/1 lb 4 oz plain flour

1. To prepare the gift jars, divide all of the ingredients evenly between six 475-ml/16-fl oz wide-mouthed preserving jars. Add the ingredients in layers, starting with the sugar. Place the lids on the jars and secure tightly.

2. Attach a gift tag to each jar with these instructions:

How to Bake Cherry-almond Muffins

You will need:

2 large eggs, lightly beaten

125 ml/4 fl oz milk

1 tsp vanilla extract or almond extract

115 g/4 oz unsalted butter, melted, plus extra for greasing (optional)

Preheat the oven to 180°C/350°F/Gas Mark 4 and lightly grease a 6-hole muffin tin or line with paper cases.

Transfer the muffin mix to a large bowl and stir to mix thoroughly. Put the eggs, milk and vanilla extract into a small bowl and beat together. Add the egg mixture to the dry ingredients and mix with a wooden spoon until well combined. Add the butter and stir until combined.

Scoop the batter into the prepared tin. Bake in the preheated oven for 20–22 minutes, until the tops are beginning to turn golden brown and a cocktail stick inserted into the centre of a muffin comes out clean. Remove from the oven and transfer to a wire rack to cool. Serve warm or at room temperature.

★ Cook's Tips ★

The muffin mix will keep for up to 6 months. Seal tightly and
store in a cool, dry place.

Blueberry Pancake Mix

There's no better way to wake up on a lazy Sunday than to home-made pancakes. Sweet yet tart dried blueberries and a hit of spicy cinnamon make these especially memorable.

MAKES: 6 large jars, each with sufficient mix for 2 servings

PREP TIME 10 minutes
COOK TIME No cooking

INGREDIENTS:

750 g/1 lb 10 oz plain flour

2 tbsp baking powder

1 tbsp bicarbonate of soda

1 tbsp salt

175 g/6 oz granulated sugar

1 tbsp ground cinnamon

175 g/6 oz soft light brown sugar

210 g/7½ oz dried blueberries

90 g/3¼ oz chopped pecan nuts

1. To prepare the gift jars, divide all of the ingredients evenly between six 475-ml/16-fl oz wide-mouthed preserving jars. Add the ingredients in layers, starting with the flour. Place the lids on the jars and secure tightly.

2. Attach a gift tag to each jar with these instructions:

How to prepare Blueberry Pancakes

You will need:

225 ml/8 fl oz buttermilk or milk

1 egg

1 tbsp unsalted butter, melted, plus extra for cooking the pancakes

maple syrup, to serve

Put the buttermilk and the egg into a large bowl and whisk together. Add the mix from the jar and the butter and mix together well.

Melt a little butter in a frying pan set over a medium–high heat. Ladle the batter into the hot pan, about 4 tablespoons at a time. Cook for 2–3 minutes, until the bubbles that form on the top of the batter burst, and are not immediately filled by more batter. Flip the pancake and cook on the other side for a further 2 minutes, or until golden brown. Continue until all of the batter has been used. Serve hot, drizzled with maple syrup.

★ Cook's Tips ★

The pancake mix will keep for up to 6 months. Cover tightly and
store in a cool, dry place.

71

★ Cook's Tips ★

The hot chocolate mix will keep for up to 6 months.
Cover tightly and store in a cool, dry place.

Peppermint crisp chocolate adds great flavour and a splash of colour to a classic festive treat.

Indulgent Peppermint Hot Chocolate Mix

MAKES: 6 large jars, each with sufficient mix for 6 servings

PREP TIME 10 minutes
COOK TIME No cooking

INGREDIENTS:

690 g/1 lb 8¾ oz milk powder

125 g/4½ oz cocoa powder

300 g/10½ oz sugar

250 g/9 oz peppermint crisp chocolate, chopped

1. To prepare the gift jars, divide all of the ingredients evenly between six 475-ml/16-fl oz wide-mouthed preserving jars. Add the ingredients in layers, starting with the milk powder. Place the lids on the jars and secure tightly.

2. Attach a tag to each jar with these instructions:

How to prepare Indulgent Peppermint Hot Chocolate

Pour the contents of the jar into a medium-sized bowl and mix to combine. For each serving, put 40 g/1½ oz of the mix into a mug and add 175 ml/6 fl oz hot water or milk. Stir until the mix is completely dissolved. Serve immediately.

Herbed Beer Pretzel Mix

Attach a small, decorative bag filled with coarse salt or a small jar of mustard to complete this at-home snack-making kit.

MAKES: 6 large jars, each with sufficient mix for 8 pretzels

PREP TIME 10 minutes
COOK TIME No cooking

INGREDIENTS:

1.3 kg/3 lb plain flour

2 tbsp sugar

2 tbsp plus ¾ tsp easy-blend dried yeast

4 tbsp dried thyme, rosemary, basil or oregano

3 tbsp salt

1. To prepare the gift jars, divide all of the ingredients evenly between six 475-ml/16-fl oz wide-mouthed preserving jars. Add the ingredients in layers, starting with the flour. Place the lids on the jars and secure tightly.

2. Attach a gift label to each jar with these instructions:

How to Prepare Herbed Beer Pretzels

You will need:

175 ml/6 fl oz beer, at room temperature

1 tbsp melted butter

30 g/1 oz plain flour, plus extra for dusting

1 egg yolk, beaten with 1 tbsp of water

coarse salt, for sprinkling

To prepare the pretzels, transfer the contents of the jar to a large mixing bowl. Add the beer and butter and mix until well combined. Add flour as needed, 1 tablespoon at a time, until the mixture is dry enough to knead with your hands (it should still be a bit sticky). Knead for several minutes until smooth. Place the dough in a large mixing bowl, cover with a clean tea towel and leave to stand in a warm place for about 1 hour, until the dough has doubled in size.

Preheat the oven to 220°C/425°F/Gas Mark 7 and line a large baking sheet with baking paper.

Turn out the dough onto a lightly floured board and divide into 8 pieces. Roll each piece into a ball and then into a long sausage shape about 30 cm/12 inches in length. Shape the lengths into pretzels and place on the prepared baking sheet.

★ Cook's Tips ★

The pretzel mix will keep for up to 6 months. Seal tightly
and store in a cool, dry place.

Brush the tops of the pretzels with the egg yolk mixture and sprinkle
with the salt. Bake in the preheated oven for about 25 minutes, until the
pretzels are golden brown. Remove from the oven and transfer to a wire
rack to cool. Serve warm or at room temperature.

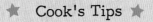

1.

2.

2.

★ Cook's Tips ★

The lentil soup mix will keep for up
to 6 months. Cover tightly and store
in a cool, dry place.

Give the gift of spicy, flavoursome home-made soup that your recipients can enjoy any time they like.

Red Lentil Soup Mix

MAKES: 6 large jars, each with sufficient mix for 4 servings

PREP TIME 10 minutes
COOK TIME No cooking

INGREDIENTS:

800 g/1 lb 12 oz dried red lentils

400 g/14 oz long-grain rice

132 g/4¾ oz sun-dried tomatoes, finely chopped

4 tbsp smoked paprika

2 tbsp sweet paprika

2 tbsp ground cumin

2 tbsp salt

1 tbsp garlic powder

1 tbsp cayenne pepper

180 g/6¼ oz chicken bouillon powder or vegetable bouillon powder

1. To prepare the gift jars, divide all of the ingredients evenly between six 475-ml/16-fl oz wide-mouthed preserving jars. Add the ingredients in layers, starting with the lentils. Place the lids on the jars and secure tightly.

2. Attach a tag to each jar with these instructions:

How to prepare Red Lentil Soup

You will need:

2 tbsp olive oil

½ onion, diced

1 carrot, diced

1 celery stick, diced

1.4 litres/2½ pints water

Heat the oil in a heavy saucepan over a medium–high heat. Add the onion and cook, stirring, for about 5 minutes until translucent. Add the carrot, celery and the contents of the jar and cook, stirring, for a further 1–2 minutes. Add the water, bring to the boil, reduce the heat to medium–low and simmer for about 30–35 minutes until the rice and lentils are cooked through. Serve hot.

Index

almonds: Cherry-Almond
Muffin Mix **66-67**
Apple Pies **20-21**
Asparagus Tarts **32-33**

Banana Splits **48-49**
beetroot: Roasted Beetroot &
Rocket Salad **52-53**
berries
Berry Cobblers **24-25**
Blueberry Pancake
Mix **70-71**
Orange Panna Cotta **42-43**
Quinoa Salads **54-55**
blackberries: Orange Panna
Cotta **42-43**
Blueberry Pancake
Mix **70-71**
bread: Olive, Sun-Dried
Tomato & Sage
Focaccia **28-29**
brownies: Double Chocolate
Brownie Mix **64-65**

cakes
Chocolate Peanut Butter
Cupcakes **40-41**
Double Chocolate Brownie
Mix **64-65**
Gingersnap Refrigerator
Cakes **44-45**
Lemon Drizzle **16-17**
Rainbow Cakes **14-15**
Red Velvet Cakes **38-39**
S'mores Cakes **18-19**

cheese
Asparagus Tarts **32-33**
Macaroni Cheese **26-27**
Pizza Margherita **30-31**
Quinoa Salads **54-55**
Roasted Beetroot & Rocket
Salad **52-53**
cherries
Banana Splits **48-49**
Cherry-Almond Muffin
Mix **66-67**
chocolate
Banana Splits **48-49**
Chocolate Chip Coconut
Cookies **60-61**
Chocolate Peanut Butter
Cupcakes **40-41**
Double Chocolate Brownie
Mix **64-65**
Indulgent Peppermint Hot
Chocolate Mix **72-73**
Red Velvet Cakes **38-39**
S'mores Cakes **18-19**
Christmas Ginger
Thins **62-63**
coconut: Chocolate Chip
Coconut Cookies **60-61**
cookies
Chocolate Chip Coconut
Cookies **60-61**
Christmas Ginger
Thins **62-63**

cream
Asparagus Tarts **32-33**
Banana Splits **48-49**
Berry Cobblers **24-25**
Cherry-Almond Muffin
Mix **66-67**
Chocolate Peanut Butter
Cupcakes **40-41**
Macaroni Cheese **26-27**

desserts
Apple Pies **20-21**
Banana Splits **48-49**
Berry Cobblers **24-25**
Chocolate Peanut Butter
Cupcakes **40-41**
Orange Panna Cotta **42-43**
drinks
Indulgent Peppermint Hot
Chocolate Mix **72-73**
Mojitos to Go **50-51**

Focaccia, Olive, Sun-Dried
Tomato & Sage **28-29**

gifts
Blueberry Pancake
Mix **70-71**
Cherry-Almond Muffin
Mix **66-67**
Chocolate Chip Coconut
Cookies **60-61**
Christmas Ginger
Thins **62-63**
Double Chocolate Brownie
Mix **64-65**

Herbed Beer Pretzel
    Mix **74-75**
Indulgent Peppermint Hot
    Chocolate Mix **72-73**
Red Lentil Soup Mix **76-77**
ginger
    Cherry-Almond Muffin
        Mix **66-67**
    Christmas Ginger
        Thins **62-63**
    Gingersnap Refrigerator
        Cakes **44-45**

hazelnuts: Double Chocolate
    Brownie Mix **64-65**
Herbed Beer Pretzel
    Mix **74-75**
honey
    Quinoa Salads **54-55**
    Roasted Beetroot & Rocket
        Salad **52-53**

ice cream: Banana Splits **48-49**

jars **5-8**
    cleaning and sterilizing **7**
    cooking in jars **12**
    freezing food in jars **5, 8, 12**
    layering ingredients **36**
    lids **5**
    mason jars **5**
    sizes **5**
    wide-mouthed jars **5, 8**

lemons
    Asparagus Tarts **32-33**
    Cherry-Almond Muffin
        Mix **66-67**
    Gingersnap Refrigerator
        Cakes **44-45**
    Lemon Drizzle **16-17**

lentils: Red Lentil Soup
    Mix **76-77**

limes: Mojitos to Go **50-51**

Macaroni Cheese **26-27**
marshmallows: S'mores
    Cakes **18-19**
mint
    Indulgent Peppermint Hot
        Chocolate Mix **72-73**
    Mojitos to Go **50-51**
    Quinoa Salads **54-55**
Mojitos to Go **50-51**
muffins: Cherry-Almond Muffin
    Mix **66-67**

nuts
    Banana Splits **48-49**
    Blueberry Pancake
        Mix **70-71**
    Cherry-Almond Muffin
        Mix **66-67**
    Chocolate Peanut Butter
        Cupcakes **40-41**
    Double Chocolate Brownie
        Mix **64-65**
    Quinoa Salads **54-55**
    Roasted Beetroot & Rocket
        Salad **52-53**

Olive, Sun-Dried Tomato & Sage
    Focaccia **28-29**
oranges
    Orange Panna Cotta **42-43**
    Roasted Beetroot & Rocket
        Salad **52-53**

pancakes: Blueberry Pancake
    Mix **70-71**
pasta: Macaroni Cheese **26-27**

pastry
    Apple Pies **20-21**
    Asparagus Tarts **32-33**

peanut butter: Chocolate
    Peanut Butter
        Cupcakes **40-41**
pecan nuts
    Blueberry Pancake
        Mix **70-71**
    Roasted Beetroot & Rocket
        Salad **52-53**
pistachio nuts: Quinoa
    Salads **54-55**
Pizza Margherita **30-31**
pretzels: Herbed Beer Pretzel
    Mix **74-75**

Quinoa Salads **54-55**

Red Velvet Cakes **38-39**
rice
    Chocolate Chip Coconut
        Cookies **60-61**
    Red Lentil Soup Mix **76-77**
rocket: Roasted Beetroot &
    Rocket Salad **52-53**

salads
    Quinoa Salads **54-55**
    Roasted Beetroot & Rocket
        Salad **52-53**
S'mores Cakes **18-19**
soups: Red Lentil Soup
    Mix **76-77**
strawberries: Quinoa
    Salads **54-55**

tomatoes
    Olive, Sun-Dried Tomato &
        Sage Focaccia **28-29**
    Pizza Margherita **30-31**
    Red Lentil Soup Mix **76-77**

walnuts: Roasted Beetroot &
    Rocket Salad **52-53**

This edition published by Parragon Books Ltd in 2013
LOVE FOOD is an imprint of Parragon Books Ltd

Parragon Books Ltd
Chartist House
15–17 Trim Street
Bath BA1 1HA, UK
www.parragon.com/lovefood

ISBN: 978-1-4723-2736-9

Printed in China

Project managed by Annabel King
Designed by Amy Orsborne
Photography by Mike Cooper
Home economy by Lincoln Jefferson
New recipes by Robin Donovan
Edited by Fiona Biggs

Notes for the Reader
This book uses both metric and imperial measurements. Follow the same units of measurement throughout; do not mix metric and imperial. All spoon measurements are level: teaspoons are assumed to be 5 ml, and tablespoons are assumed to be 15 ml. Unless otherwise stated, milk is assumed to be full fat, eggs and individual vegetables are medium, and pepper is freshly ground black pepper. Unless otherwise stated, all root vegetables should be washed in plain water and peeled prior to using. For best results, use a food thermometer when cooking meat and poultry – check the latest government guidelines for current advice.

Garnishes, decorations and serving suggestions are all optional and not necessarily included in the recipe ingredients or method. The times given are an approximate guide only. Preparation times differ according to the techniques used by different people and the cooking times may also vary from those given. Optional ingredients, variations or serving suggestions have not been included in the time calculations.

Recipes using raw or very lightly cooked eggs should be avoided by infants, the elderly, pregnant women, convalescents and anyone suffering from an illness. Pregnant and breastfeeding women are advised to avoid eating peanuts and peanut products. Sufferers from nut allergies should be aware that some of the ready-made ingredients used in the recipes in this book may contain nuts. Always check the packaging before use. Vegetarians should be aware that some of the ready-made ingredients used in the recipes in this book may contain animal products. Always check the packaging before use. Please consume alcohol responsibly.